CHANNEL ISLANDS
NATIONAL PARK
ACTIVITY BOOK

PUZZLES, MAZES, GAMES, AND MORE ABOUT
CHANNEL ISLANDS NATIONAL PARK

NATIONAL PARKS ACTIVITIES SERIES

CHANNEL ISLANDS NATIONAL PARK ACTIVITY BOOK

Copyright 2022
Published by Little Bison Press

The author acknowledges that the land on which Channel Islands National Park is located are the traditional lands of Chumash, Limuw, and Michumash Tribes.

LITTLE BISON
Press

For more free national parks activities, visit
www.littlebisonpress.com

About Channel Islands National Park

Channel Islands National Park is located off the coast of Southern California. While there is a visitors center on the mainland, the rest of the park can only be accessed by boat.

Given national park status in 1980, the park is famous for encompassing five remarkable islands: **San Miguel, Santa Rosa, Santa Cruz, Anacapa,** and **Santa Barbara,** as well as their ocean environment. The isolated location of the park is what helps make this place unique. Due to it being so far from the mainland, the islands' natural and cultural resources have been protected. Over time, this has shaped animals, plants, and archeological resources. Some living creatures on the Channel Islands are found nowhere else on Earth!

After their boat ride, visitors can explore the islands by hiking, camping, birding, kayaking, and tide pooling. Some people even brave the cold water conditions and go snorkeling or diving. This park is primitive—there are no grocery stores, restaurants, or hotels on the islands, so visitors must plan well and be prepared for the adventure!

Channel Islands National Park is famous for:
- five isolated islands
- plants and animals that live nowhere else in the world
- hiking, camping, birding, kayaking, and tide pooling

Hey, I'm Parker!

I'm the only snail in history to visit every National Park in the United States! Come join me on my adventures in Channel Islands National Park.

Throughout this book, we will learn about the history of the park, the animals and plants that live here, and things to do if you ever visit in person. This book is also full of games and activities!

Last but not least, I am hidden 9 times on different pages. See how many times you can find me. This page doesn't count!

Channel Islands Bingo

Let's play bingo! Cross off each box you are able to during your visit to the national park. Try to get a bingo down, across, or diagonally. If you can't visit the park, use the bingo board to plan your perfect trip.

Pick out some activities you would want to do during your visit. What would you do first? How long would you spend there? What animals would you try to see?

SPOT A SEA LION	SEE A PELICAN	GO FOR A HIKE	TAKE A PICTURE AT AN OVERLOOK	WATCH A MOVIE AT THE VISITORS CENTER
IDENTIFY A TREE	LEARN ABOUT THE INDIGENOUS PEOPLE WHO LIVE IN THIS AREA	WITNESS A SUNRISE OR SUNSET	OBSERVE THE NIGHT SKIES	GO TIDEPOOLING
HEAR A BIRD CALL	SPOT AN ARCH ROCK	FREE SPACE	LEARN ABOUT THE ISLAND GRAY FOX	SPOT SOME ANIMAL TRACKS
PICK UP TEN PIECES OF TRASH	HAVE A PICNIC	SEE A SEAL	VISIT A LIGHTHOUSE	SPOT A BIRD OF PREY
LEARN ABOUT THE GEOLOGY OF THE ISLANDS	SEE SOMEONE SURFING	TAKE A BOAT RIDE	VISIT A RANGER STATION	PARTICIPATE IN A RANGER-LED ACTIVITY

Draw a Fox

Complete the picture below by drawing the other half of the fox. Complete the image by coloring it in.

Channel Islands National Park is home to the Island fox. This animal is among only 4 native mammals on the islands. The others include the island deer mouse, the harvest mouse, and the spotted skunk.

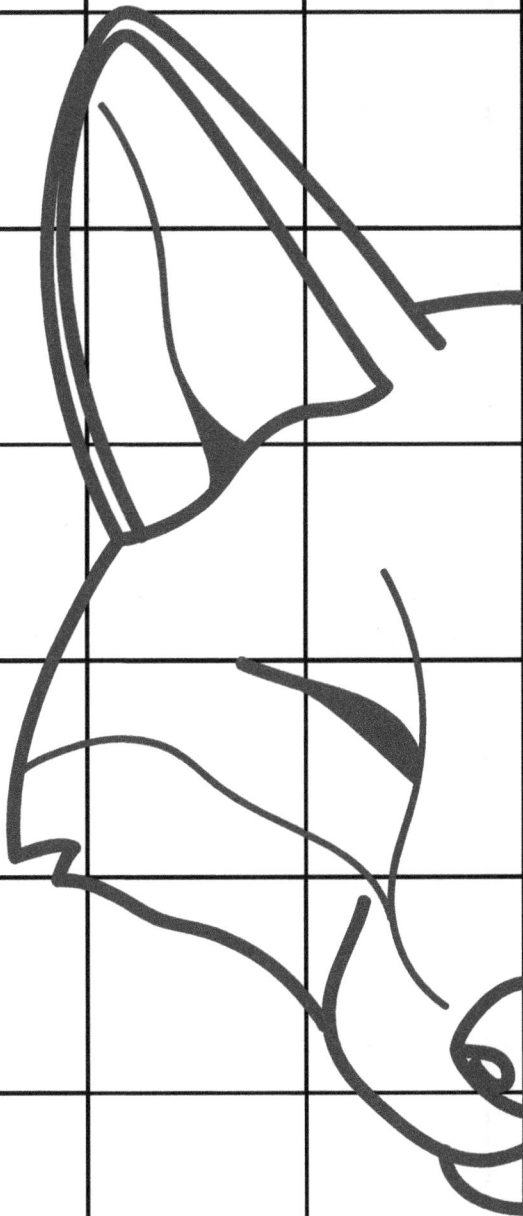

Take a Hike

Go for a hike with your friends or family. If you aren't able to visit Channel Islands National Park, go for a walk in a park near where you live. Read through the prompts before your walk and finish the activities after you return.

Draw something you saw that moves:

Draw something you saw when you looked up:

Draw something you saw that grows out of the ground:

Draw a picture of your favorite part of the walk:

Hidden Picture

After a long day of exploring the park, you might find your way to lower elevations to use something like this.

4	4	4	4	4	4	4	4	4	1	4 / 1	4
4	4	4	4	4	4	4	4	4	4	1	4
4	4	4	4	4	4	4	4	4	4	1	4
4	2	2	2	2	4 / 2	2	2	2	2	1	4
4	2	5	5	5	5	5	5	5	2	1	4
2	2	5	5	5 / 2	2	2 / 5	5	5	2	2	4
4	2	5	5	2	2 / 4	2	5	5	2	1	4
4	2	2	2	2	4	2	2	2	2	1	4
4	4	4	4	4	4	4	4	4	4	1 / 3	4
4	4	4	4	3 / 4	4	3 / 4	4	4	4	1 / 3	4
4	4	4	4	3 / 4	4 / 3	3 / 4	4	4	4 / 1 / 3	1	4
4	4	4	4	4	3	1	1	3	1	3	1 / 3 / 1	4

Directions:

You will need crayons or colored pencils in each of the listed colors. Use the color code to help you figure out what the hidden picture is. For example, you will color every square with the number 4 dark blue. Some squares will call for more than one color.

1-Red
2-Yellow
3-Black
4-Dark Blue
5-Light Blue

Surf the Waves on Santa Rosa Island

start
here →

DID YOU KNOW?
Surfing is an adventurous way to explore Channel Islands National Park. All surf spots are remote and best accessed by private boat.

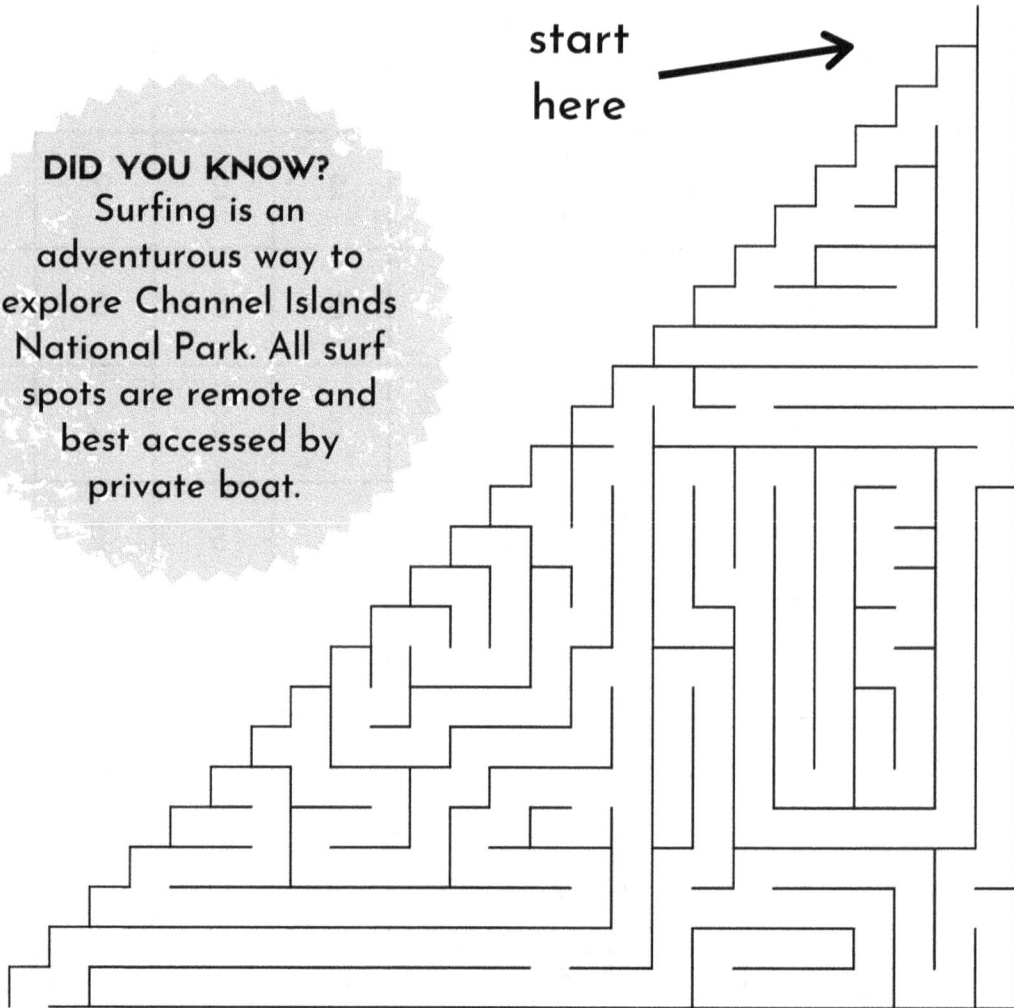

Camping Packing List

What should you take with you when you go camping? Pretend you are in charge of your family camping trip. Make a list of what you would need to be safe and comfortable on an overnight excursion. Some considerations are listed on the side.

1.
2.
3.
4.
5.
6.
7.
8.
9.
10.
11.
12.
13.
14.
15.
16.

- What will you eat at every meal?

- What will the weather be like?

- Where will you sleep?

- What will you do during your free time?

- How luxurious do you want your camp to be?

- How will you cook?

- How will you see at night?

- How will you dispose of trash?

- What might you need in case of emergencies?

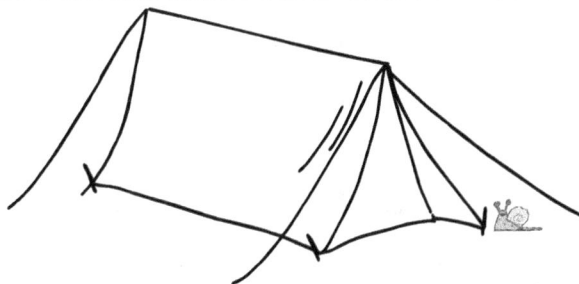

Camping at Channel Islands NP is not for the faint of heart! You will need to store all your food in animal-proof containers. This includes protection from birds too, as some ravens in the park know how to un-do zippers in order to get food!

Channel Islands National Park

Visitor's Log

Date: _____

Season: _____

Who I went with: _____

Which island: _____

How was your experience? Write a few sentences about your trip. What was the boat ride like? What did you do? What was your favorite activity? If you haven't visited the park yet, write a paragraph pretending that you did.

_____

_____

_____

_____

_____

STAMPS

Many national parks and monuments have cancellation stamps for visitors to use. These rubber stamps record the date and location that you visited. Many people collect the markings as a free souvenir. Check with a ranger to see where you can find a stamp during your visit. If you aren't able to find one, you can draw your own.

Where is the Park?

Channel Islands National Park is in the western United States. It is located off the coast of Southern California. The park includes 5 of the 8 Channel Islands. San Clemente, Santa Catalina, and San Nicolas are the other three islands that are not part of the park.

California

Look at the shape of California. Can you find it on the map? If you are from the US, can you find your home state? Color California red. Put a star on the map where you live.

Connect the Dots #1

Connect the dots to figure out what this tiny critter is. There are six types of these that live in Channel Islands National Park.

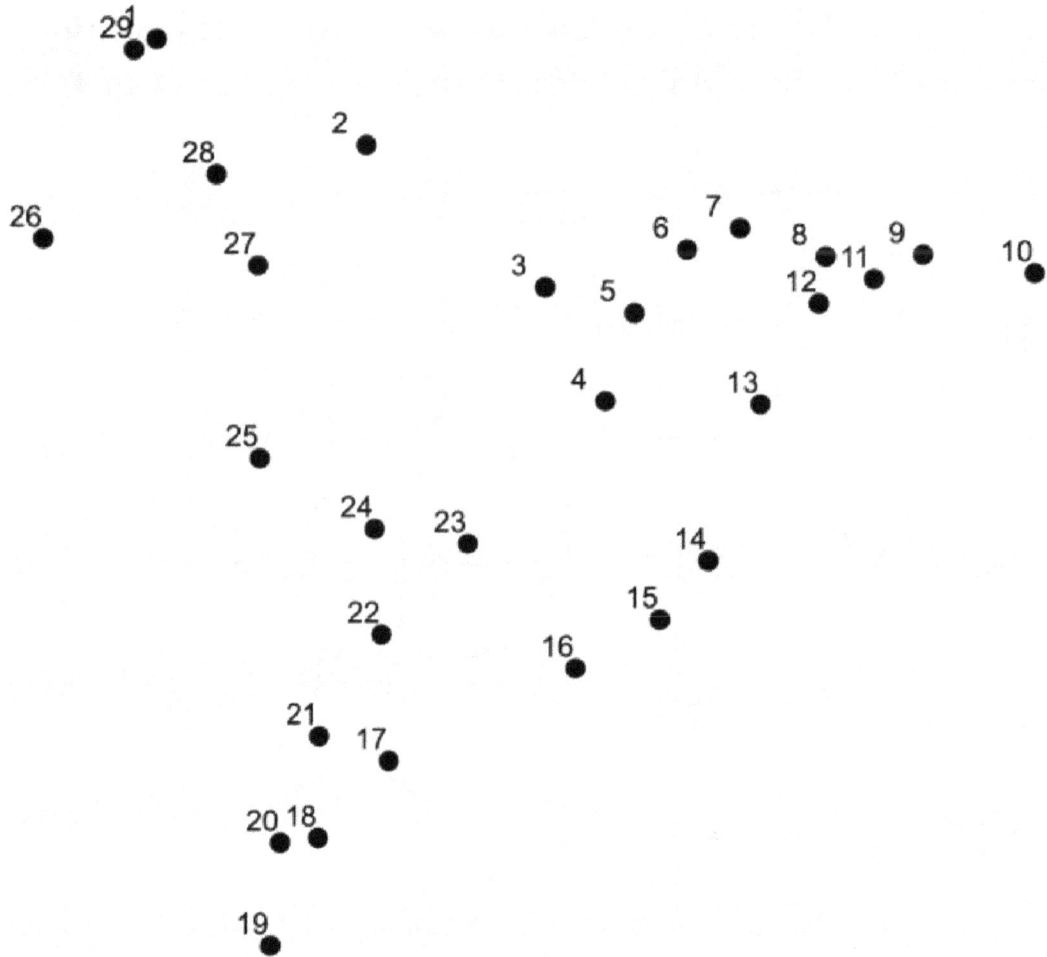

29 1
2
28
26
27
3
6 7
8 11 9
10
12
5
4
13
25
24 23
14
22
15
16
21 17
20 18
19

Their heart rate can reach as high as 1,260 beats per minute and a breathing rate of 250 breaths per minute. Have you ever measured your breathing rate? Ask a friend or family member to set a timer for 60 seconds. Once they say "go," try to breathe normally. Count each breath until they say "stop." How do your breaths per minute compare to hummingbirds?

_____

_____

Bird Scavenger Hunt

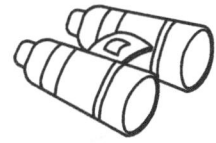

Channel Islands National Park is a great place to go birdwatching. You don't have to be able to identify different species of birds in order to have fun. Open your eyes and tune in your ears. Check off as many birds on this list as you can.

☐ A colorful bird   ☐ A big bird

☐ A brown bird   ☐ A small bird

☐ A bird in a tree   ☐ A hopping bird

☐ A bird with long tail feathers   ☐ A flying bird

☐ A bird making noise   ☐ A bird's nest

☐ A bird eating or hunting   ☐ A bird's footprint on the ground

☐ A bird with spots   ☐ A bird with stripes

What was the easiest bird on the list to find? What was the hardest?
Why do you think that was?

_____

_____

_____

Who Lives Here?

Below are 7 plants and animals that live in the park.
Use the word bank to fill in the clues below.

WORD BANK: GEODUCK, GRAY WHALE, OSPREY, LIMPET,
BULL KELP, VERBENA, KESTREL

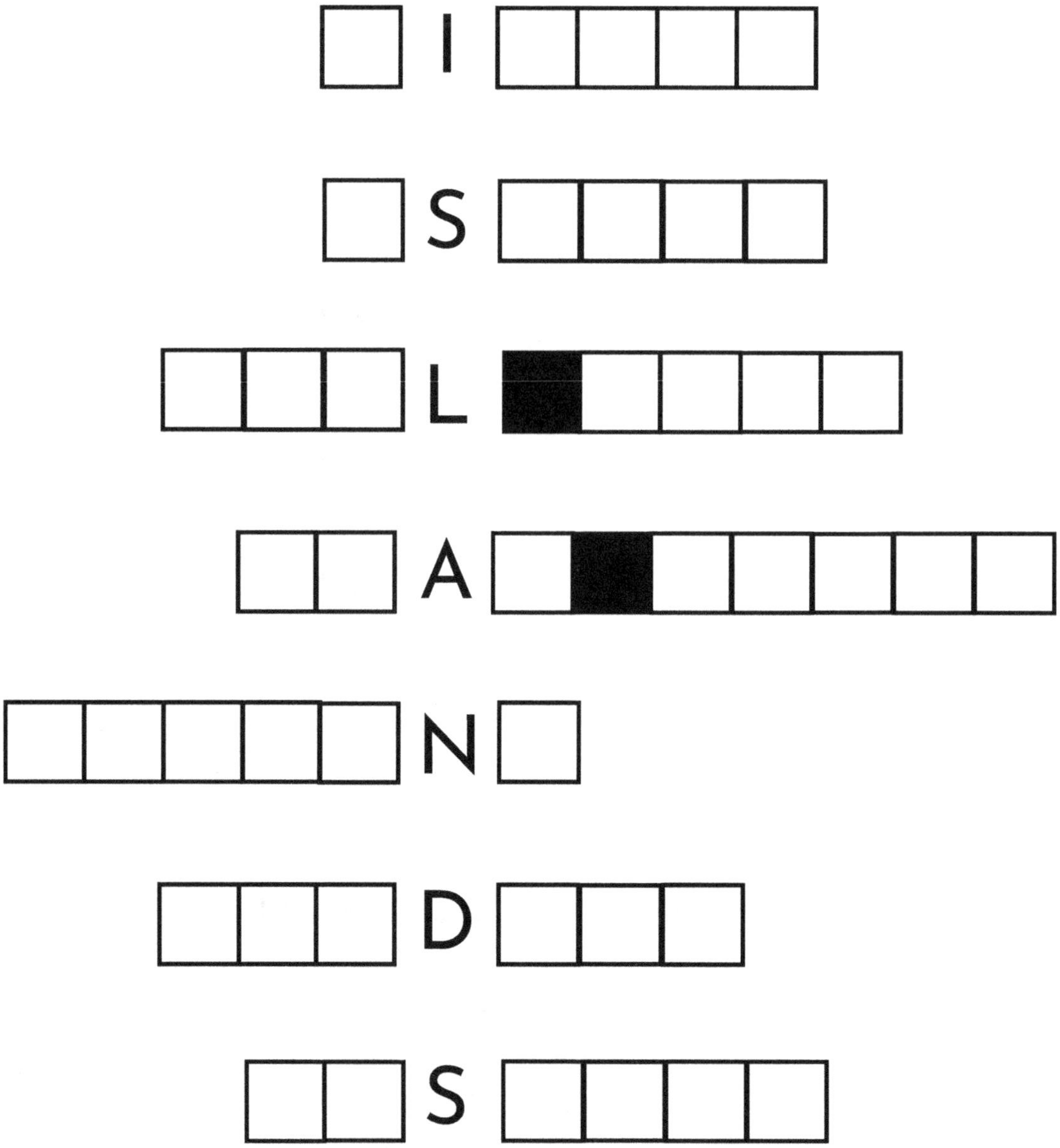

☐ I ☐ ☐ ☐

☐ S ☐ ☐ ☐

☐ ☐ L ■ ☐ ☐ ☐

☐ ☐ A ☐ ■ ☐ ☐ ☐ ☐

☐ ☐ ☐ ☐ N ☐

☐ ☐ D ☐ ☐

☐ ☐ S ☐ ☐ ☐

Animals of Channel Islands National Park

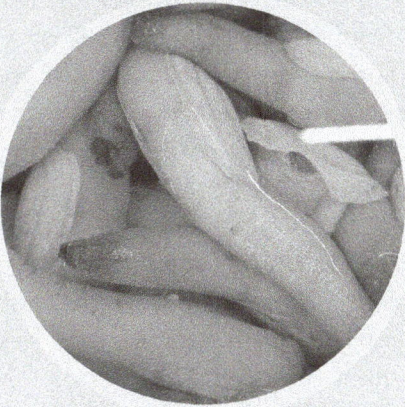

Geoducks
(Pronounced gooey-duck) are large clams. They can weigh up to 7 lbs!

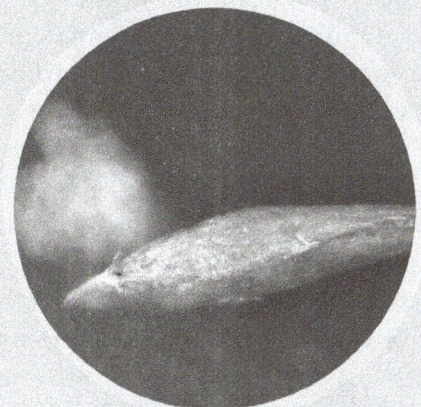

Gray Whale
is a baleen whale that migrates between feeding and breeding grounds yearly.

Osprey
can be found on every continent except Antarctica.

Kestrel
is the smallest falcon in North America.

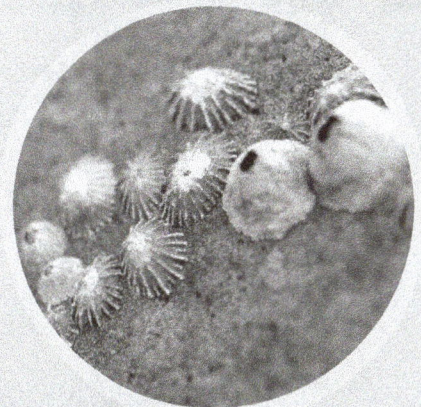

Limpet
is a marine mollusk that is usually found clinging to rocks.

Common Names
vs.
Scientific Names

A common name of an organism is a name that is based on everyday language. You have heard the common names of plants, animals, and other living things on tv, in books, and at school. Common names can also be referred to as "English" names, popular names, or farmer's names. Common names can vary from place to place. The word for a particular tree may be one thing, but that same tree has a different name in another country. Common names can even vary from region to region, even in the same country.

Scientific names, or Latin names, are given to organisms to make it possible to have uniform names for the same species. Scientific names are in Latin. You may have heard plants or animals referred to by their scientific name or parts of their scientific names. Latin names are also called "binomial nomenclature," which refers to a two-part naming system. The first part of the name - the generic name - refers to the genus to which the species belongs. The second part of the name, the specific name, identifies the species. For example, Tyrannosaurus rex is an example of a widely known scientific name.

COMMON NAME

Sea Otter
Enhydra lutris

Harbor Seal
Phoca vitulina

LATIN NAME = GENUS + SPECIES

Sea Otter = Enhydra lutris

Harbor Seal = Phoca vitulina

Find the Match!
Common Names and Latin Names

Match the common name to the scientific name for each animal. The first one is done for you. Use clues on the page before and after this one to complete the matches.

Channel Island Gray Fox

California Sagebrush

Island Oak

California Sea Lion

Great Horned Owl

Bald Eagle

Northern Elephant Seal

Green Sea Turtle

Side-blotched Lizard

Haliaeetus leucocephalus

Zalophus californianus

Mirounga angustirostris

Chelonia mydas

Artemisia californica

Uta stansburiana

Bubo virginianus

Urocyon littoralis

Quercus tomentella

Bald Eagle

Haliaeetus leucocephalus

Channel Island Gray Fox
Urocyon littoralis

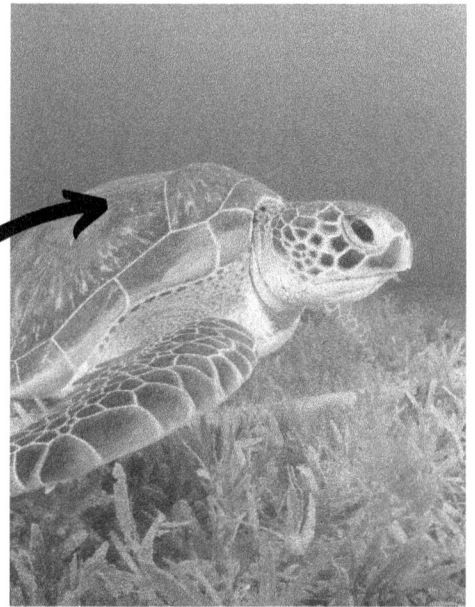

Green Sea Turtle
Chelonia mydas

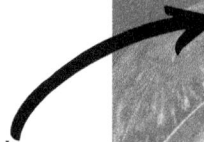

Great Horned Owl
Bubo virginianus

Some plants and animals that live at Channel Islands

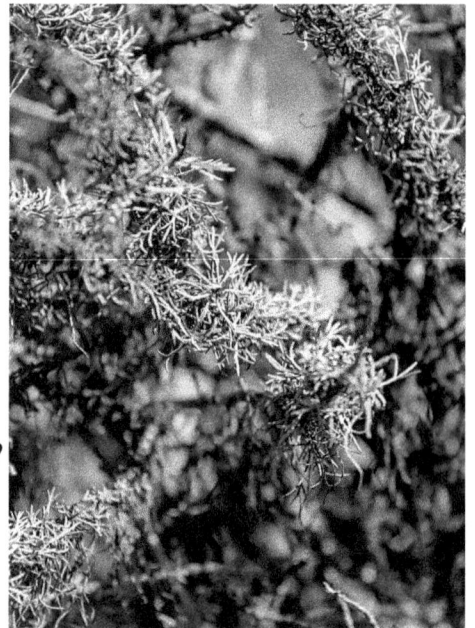

California Sagebrush
Artemisia californica

Northern Elephant Seal
Mirounga angustirostris

Side-blotched Lizard
Uta stansburiana

Things To Do Jumble

Unscramble the letters to uncover activities you can do while in Channel Islands National Park. Hint: each one ends in -ing.

1. BTOA ◻◻◻◻ING

2. IHK ◻◻◻ING

3. DBIR ◻◻◻◻ING

4. MACP ◻◻◻◻ING

5. KINICPC ◻◻◻◻◻◻◻ING

6. EISSTEHG ◻◻◻◻◻◻◻◻ING

7. NORSLEK ◻◻◻◻◻◻◻ING

Word Bank

birding
reading
camping
snorkeling
horseback riding
hiking
surfing
singing
boating
sightseeing
picnicking

Animal Movements

Pretend to be some of the creatures that spend time in Channel Islands National Park. Remember to be safe while doing these activities.

Leap like a Baja California treefrog

The Baja California treefrog is a small frog that lives on Santa Cruz, Santa Rosa, and Catalina. They are predators and feed mostly on flying insects. Their songs are most often heard in spring, but they can be heard year-round.

Crouch down low with your hands flat on the ground. Then explode into a big frog jump with your arms over your head. See if you can do 8 big frog jumps.

Move like a Harbor seal

Harbor seals are agile both underwater and on land. Seals are mammals, so they cannot breathe underwater. They need to "haul out," which means to come ashore. While on the beach, they can rest, give birth or rear their pups, or molt (shed their coat).

Try to move like a seal on the beach. Lay on the ground with your arms to your sides and try to move forward. How far can you go?

Fly like a Townsend's big-eared bat

The average wingspan of one of these bats is just under 1 foot. Even though you don't have wings, your wingspan is the distance between the tips of your longest fingers when your arms are stretched out.

See how many times you can flap your arms in 30 seconds.

When Nature Calls...

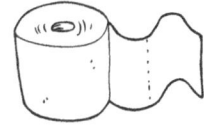

Read the following paragraph to discover the important waste management plays in our national parks. Fill in the blanks with words from the word bank, at right, as you read.

Word Bank:

flush
flow
hard
urinate
ecosystem
pit
never
ashes
plumbing
container
inches
recycling

No matter where you go, don't forget to wash your hands with soap and water afterward! At the very least, pack hand sanitizer to use.

The people who work at national parks are responsible for ensuring proper waste management from guests. Waste management isn't just about making sure trash and _____ go to the right places. It also means human waste! It may not be pleasant to think about, but all humans _____ (pee) and defecate (poop). It is important to consider how to deal with human waste to keep parks clean, safe, and with as little disturbance to the _____ as possible.

There are different types of bathrooms or methods used to deal with human waste. In visitor centers, you are likely to encounter a standard _____ toilet, which uses water and modern _____ to whisk your waste away. Near trails or at campgrounds, you may find toilets that don't flush. A _____ toilet is a type of toilet built over a hole in the ground. A composting toilet decomposes human waste into compost with an aerobic process. A vault toilet stores urine and feces in an underground _____ or vault before it is pumped out. Unlike pit toilets, they are less stinky because of vent pipes, which allow air to _____ from the vault out through the ceiling.

No matter which type of toilet you encounter, there are some things you should keep in mind to help protect the park. First, _____ put anything in the toilet other than pee, poop, or toilet paper. Things like snack wrappers, diapers, or _____ from a campfire can damage toilet systems. It can cost a lot of money and time to fix. Make sure trash goes in the trash can, not any toilet.

If you have to "go" while you are in the backcountry, here is what you should do. If you have to pee, try to urinate on a _____ surface like rocks, not plants. Animals are attracted to the salt in urine and may dig up vegetation to get to it. If you have to poop, you will need to dig a cat hole. First, select a location. It must be at least 200 feet away from any water source. Use a small shovel to dig a hole about 6 _____ deep. Do your business in the hole, then bury ONLY your poop. Take a trash bag with you, as you will need to take your toilet paper with you along with the rest of your trash. If not, animals may dig up the toilet paper which is bad for them.

The National Park Logo

The National Park System has over 400 units in the US. Just like Channel National Park, each location is unique or special in some way. The areas include other national parks, historic sites, monuments, seashores, and other recreation areas.

Each element of the National Park emblem represents something that the National Park Service protects. Fill in each blank below to show what each symbol represents.

```
WORD BANK:
MOUNTAINS, ARROWHEAD, BISON,
SEQUOIA TREE, WATER
```

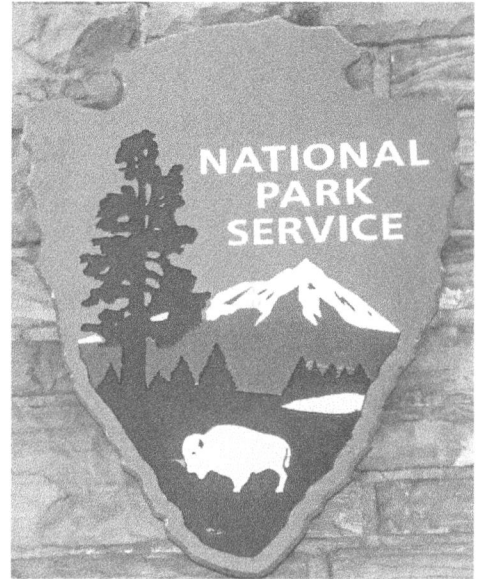

This represents all plants: _____

This represents all animals: _____

This represents the landscapes: _____

This represents the waters protected by the park service: _____

This represents the historical and archeological values: _____

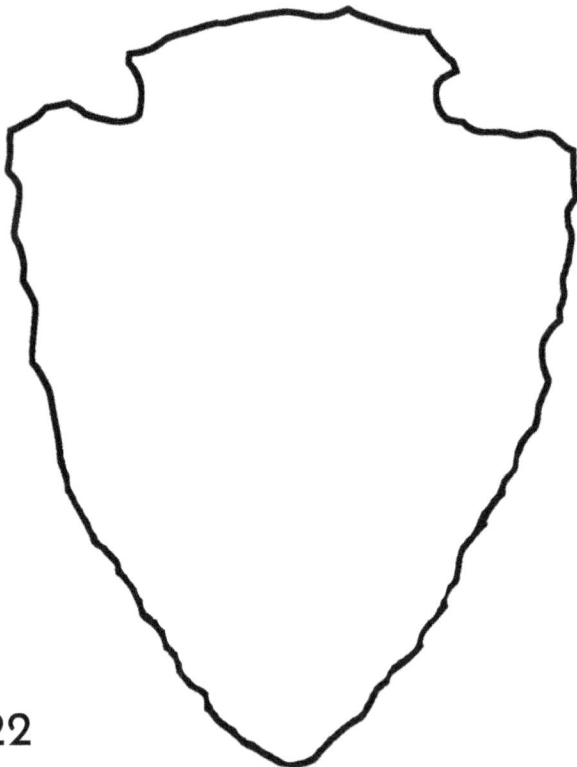

Now it's your turn! Pretend you are designing a new national park. Add elements to the design that represent the things your park protects.

What is the name of your park?

Describe why you included the symbols that you chose. What do they mean?

The Ten Essentials

Careful preparation and knowledge are key to a successful adventure when visiting Channel Islands National Park.

The ten essentials are a list of things that are important to have when you go for longer hikes. If you go on a hike to the <u>backcountry</u>, it is especially important that you have everything you need in case of an emergency. If you get lost or something unforeseen happens, it is good to be prepared to survive until help finds you.

The ten essentials list was developed in the 1930s by an outdoors group called the Mountaineers. Over time and with technological advancements, this list has evolved. Can you identify all the things on the current list? Circle each of the "essentials" and cross out everything that doesn't make the cut.

fire: matches, lighter, tinder, and/or stove	a pint of milk	extra money	headlamp, plus extra batteries	extra clothes
extra water	a dog	Polaroid camera	bug net	lightweight games, like a deck of cards
extra food	a roll of duct tape	shelter	sun protection, such as sunglasses, sun-protective clothes, and sunscreen	knife, plus a gear repair kit
a mirror	navigation: map, compass, altimeter, GPS device, or satellite messenger	first aid kit	extra flip-flops	entertainment, such as video games or books

Backcountry - a remote, undeveloped rural area.

Endemic Species of Channel Islands

Endemic species are those that exist in only one location or area on Earth. A total of 23 endemic terrestrial species have been identified in the park, including 11 land birds that are Channel Island subspecies.

Channel Island Gray Fox

Deer Mouse
(each of the 5 channel islands has its own subspecies)

Channel Islands House Finch

Draw Your Own!
Use your imagination to create a new species.

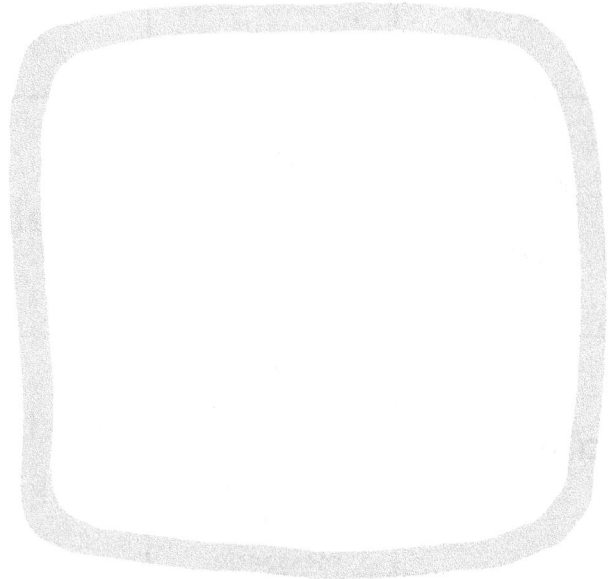

Don't forget to give it a name! _____

Channel Islands Word Search

Words may be horizontal, vertical, diagonal,
or they might even be backwards!

1. MARINE
2. SEAWEED
3. SEALIONS
4. CALIFORNIA
5. FOX
6. GRASSLAND
7. CHUMASH
8. TOMOLS
9. FISHING
10. SANTA CRUZ
11. DEVILS PEAK
12. SCUBA
13. WHALE WATCH
14. STAIRCASE
15. LIZARDS
16. BOATRIDE
17. CHARTER
18. SEA
19. PACIFIC
20. CLIFFS

```
C A L I F O R N I A R E S K S
H T A T M I L E S H E R W R A
T E S E A W E E D C L B R P N
S M P A S P R U D E R L E A T
C E A I I E R N Q E I N T C A
H O L D Y W A O E B I E R I O
U O A D P L E G S R T R A F R
M W B A S E I N A W E I H I A
A A H S G E L M C E E D C C N
S L A C B O A T R I D E O T R
H R A U A C I L I Z A R D S A
G C N B K M O I A O B K G R E
I W H A L E W A T C H A N F D
J Y G T O M O L S O O R I O O
N W X A K C L I F F S O H X M
S A N T A C R U Z L Z E S Q N
U A E S E A L I O N S P I E B
D E V I L S P E A K M A F A S
```

25

Wildlife Wisdom

The national park is home to many different kinds of animals. Seeing wildlife can be an exciting part of visiting the national park but it is important to remember that these animals are wild. They need plenty of space and a healthy habitat where they can find their own food. Part of this is not allowing animals to eat any human food. This is their home and we are the visitors. We need to be respectful of the wildlife in the park.

Directions: Circle the highlighted words that best complete the following sentences.

If an animal changes its behavior because of your presence, you are:
  A) too close
  B) funny looking
  C) dehydrated and should drink more water

The best thing we can do to help wild animals survive is:
  A) make them pets
  B) protect their habitat
  C) knit them winter sweaters

In a national park, it is okay to share your food with wild animals:
  A) never
  B) always
  C) sometimes

When you're hiking in an area where there are bears, you should warn bears that you are entering their space by:
  A) hiking quietly
  B) making noise
  C) wearing bright colors

At night, park rangers care for the animals by:
  A) putting them back into their cages
  B) tucking them into bed
  C) leaving them alone

If you see an abandoned bird's nest, it is best to:
  A) pet the baby birds
  B) leave it alone
  C) crunch the empty eggshells

Spotted skunks forage along the ground in hopes of finding:
  A) granola bars
  B) Jerusalem crickets
  C) peanuts to eat

The place where an animal lives is called its:
  A) condo
  B) habitat
  C) crib

Park Poetry

America's parks inspire art of all kinds. Painters, sculptors, photographers, writers, and artists of all mediums have taken inspiration from natural beauty. They have turned their inspiration into great works.

Use this space to write your own poem about the park. Think about what you have experienced or seen. Use descriptive language to create an acrostic poem. This type of poem has the first letter of each line spell out another word. Create an acrostic that spells out the word "Island."

I _____

S _____

L _____

A _____

N _____

D _____

I mpressive

S unrise

L ow tide

A nemones all around

N othing but ocean

D ont want to leave

I ntertidal

S ea creatures

L impets

A ll around

N ew

D iscoveries

27

The Perfect Picnic Spot

Fill in the blanks on this page without looking at the full story. Once you have each line filled out, use the words you've chosen to complete the story on the next page.

EMOTION _____

FOOD _____

SOMETHING SWEET _____

STORE _____

MODE OF TRANSPORTATION _____

NOUN _____

SOMETHING ALIVE _____

SAUCE _____

PLURAL VEGETABLES _____

ADJECTIVE _____

PLURAL BODY PART _____

ANIMAL _____

PLURAL FRUIT _____

PLACE _____

SOMETHING TALL _____

COLOR _____

ADJECTIVE _____

NOUN _____

A DIFFERENT ANIMAL _____

FAMILY MEMBER #1 _____

FAMILY MEMBER #2 _____

VERB THAT ENDS IN -ING _____

A DIFFERENT FOOD _____

The Perfect Picnic Spot

Use the words from the previous page to complete a silly story.

When my family suggested having our lunch at Water Canyon Beach, I was

_ _ _ _ _ _ _ _. I love eating my _ _ _ _ _ _ outside! I knew we had picked up a
EMOTION   FOOD

box of _ _ _ _ _ _ from the _ _ _ _ _ _ _ _ for after lunch, my favorite. We drove up
SOMETHING SWEET   STORE

to the area and I jumped out of the _ _ _ _ _ _ _ _ _. "I will find the perfect spot for
                                    MODE OF TRANSPORTATION

a picnic!" I grabbed a _ _ _ _ _ _ for us to sit on, and I ran off. I passed a picnic
                        NOUN

table, but it was covered with _ _ _ _ _ _ _ _ so we couldn't sit there. The next
                               SOMETHING ALIVE

picnic table looked okay, but there were smears of _ _ _ _ _ _ _ and pieces of
                                                    SAUCE

_ _ _ _ _ _ _ _ everywhere. The people that were there before must have been
PLURAL VEGETABLES

_ _ _ _ _ _! I gritted my _ _ _ _ _ _ _ together and kept walking down the path,
ADJECTIVE   PLURAL BODY PART

determined to find the perfect spot. I wanted a table with a good view of the

ocean. Why was this so hard? If we were lucky, I might even get to see _ _ _ _ _ _
                                                                       ANIMAL

eating some _ _ _ _ _ _ on the cliffside. They don't have those in _ _ _ _ _ _ _, where
            PLURAL FRUIT   PLACE

I am from. I walked down a little hill and there it was, the perfect spot! The

trees towered overhead and looked as tall as _ _ _ _ _ _ _ _. The patch of grass
                                             SOMETHING TALL

was a beautiful _ _ _ _ _ _ _ color. The _ _ _ _ _ _ flowers were growing on
                COLOR   ADJECTIVE

the side of a _ _ _ _ _ _ _. I looked across the cliffs edge and even saw a
              NOUN

_ _ _ _ _ _ _ _ on the edge of a rock. I looked back to see my _ _ _ _ _ _ _ _ _ and
DIFFERENT ANIMAL   FAMILY MEMBER #1

_ _ _ _ _ _ _ _ _ _ _ _ _ _ _ _ _ a picnic basket. "I hope you brought plenty of
FAMILY MEMBER #2   VERB THAT ENDS IN ING

_ _ _ _ _ _ _ _, I'm starving!"
A DIFFERENT FOOD

29

Hike to the Beach

start
here →

DID YOU KNOW?

Each of the Channel Islands
is fringed by miles of coastal
beaches, dunes, wetlands,
lagoons, caves, and rocky
intertidal areas.

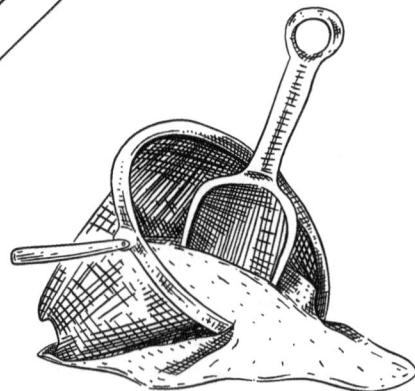

Design a Sweatshirt

Imagine you are a graphic designer and you have been hired to design a sweatshirt that will be for sale in the Robert J. Lagomarsino Visitor Center. Use your knowledge of Channel Islands National Park to create a meaningful souvenir.

Your design should include:

- the name of the park
- the year the park was established
- 2 or more colors that represent the park
- 1 symbol or feature of the park

Use colored pencils, crayons, or markers to make your designs. You can include artwork on the sleeves too!

Leave No Trace Quiz

Leave No Trace is a concept that helps people make decisions during outdoor recreation that protects the environment. There are seven principles that guide us when we spend time outdoors, whether you are in a national park or not. Are you an expert in Leave No Trace? Take this quiz and find out!

1. How can you plan ahead and prepare to ensure you have the best experience you can in the national park?
   a. Make sure you stop by the ranger station for a map and to ask about current conditions.
   b. Just wing it! You will know the best trail when you see it.
   c. Stick to your plan, even if conditions change. You traveled a long way to get here, and you should stick to your plan.
2. What is an example of traveling on a durable surface?
   a. Walking only on the designated path.
   b. Walking on the grass that borders the trail if the trail is very muddy.
   c. Taking a shortcut if you can find one because it means you will be walking less.
3. Why should you dispose of waste properly?
   a. You don't need to. Park rangers love to pick up the trash you leave behind.
   b. You should actually leave your leftovers behind, because animals will eat them. It is important to make sure they aren't hungry.
   c. So that other peoples' experiences of the park are not impacted by you leaving your waste behind.
4. How can you best follow the concept "leave what you find?"
   a. Take only a small rock or leaf to remember your trip.
   b. Take pictures, but leave any physical items where they are.
   c. Leave everything you find, unless it may be rare like an arrowhead, then it is okay to take.
5. What is not a good example of minimizing campfire impacts?
   a. Only having a campfire in a pre-existing campfire ring.
   b. Checking in with current conditions when you consider making a campfire.
   c. Building a new campfire ring in a location that has a better view.
6. What is a poor example of respecting wildlife?
   a. Building squirrel houses out of rocks so the squirrels have a place to live.
   b. Stay far away from wildlife and give them plenty of space.
   c. Reminding your grown-ups not to drive too fast in animal habitats while visiting the park.
7. How can you show consideration of other visitors?
   a. Play music on your speaker so other people at the campground can enjoy it.
   b. Wear headphones on the trail if you choose to listen to music.
   c. Make sure to yell "Hello!" to every animal you see at top volume.

Tide Pool Word Search

A tide pool is an isolated pocket of seawater found in the intertidal zone. They are packed with resilient sea life. Be sure to check out tide-pooling etiquette before exploring!

1. ANEMONE
2. FRENCHYS
3. TRANSITION
4. INTERTIDAL
5. URCHINS
6. SUNLIGHT
7. ALGAE
8. ROCKS
9. SMUGGLERS
10. SEA STAR
11. WAVES
12. PERIWINKLES
13. BEACH
14. BARNACLES
15. MUSSELS
16. LIMPETS
17. HIGH TIDE
18. LOW TIDE
19. BECHERS BAY

```
B E C H E R S B A Y K L U W I
H L O W T I D E R T E R R R N
T E P S E L C A N R A B C N T
S M P A S P S U C E U L H O E
C E A A L G A E S E R U I I R
B E A C H W O O V B C E N T T
R O R O C K S G A A H R S I I
P W B L M E I N G W W I K S D
P E R I W I N K L E S E S N A
E N I M A B O Y H I N G O A L
Q O A P A C I T N N S E N R N
S M N E S Y H C N E R F I T E
I E O T F G B T A H F A Q N D
J N G S I E V S S O O R V E O
N A X L K C T B S L E S S U M
X J N F A A H I G H T I D E N
U U E E R S E N N E T P V E B
S J S M U G G L E R S M A L S
```

There are many places in the Channel Islands where you can explore tidepools including Frenchy's Cove on Anacapa Island, Smuggler's Cove on Santa Cruz Island, and East Point on Santa Rosa Island.

Tide Pool Etiquette

Tide-pooling is a unique activity that you can do during low tides. It can be as simple as walking on the beach and observing what you see in the pools of water left by the ocean. Follow these tips to show your respect for life at the water's edge.

1. Bring a bag on your beach outing to pick up any garbage or small pieces of plastic you find.

2. Look for footholds on bare rock. Bare patches are less slippery and you won't step on the animals and plants that cling to these surfaces.

3. Keep one foot on the ground at all times. Stepping carefully from rock to rock keeps both you and the critters safe.

4. When you look under a rock, put it back the way it was when you're done. Leaving a rock upside down can kill any animals that were living on its underside.

5. Tide pool animals should not be collected or used for fishing bait.

6. Don't build driftwood campfires. They can smolder unseen within the sand for many weeks.

7. Rough handling hurts intertidal animals. Never force an animal off its spot. You may rip its feet off or squeeze its organs and hurt it.

8. Respect animals' "body language." An animal that resists being removed from a surface will cling more tightly. Let it stay safe where it is.

Tide Pool Observation

Draw a picture of yourself or someone else on the beach using good tide pool etiquette. Don't forget to add some intertidal animals to your drawing. Use the words from page 33 for ideas.

Which of the tide pool etiquette tips are shown in your drawing? What critters did you draw in your tide pool?

_____

_____

_____

Stacking Rocks

Have you ever seen stacks of rocks while hiking in national parks? Do you know what they are or what they mean? These rock piles are called cairns and often mark hiking routes in parks. Every park has a different way to maintain trails and cairns. However, they all have the same rule: If you come across a cairn, do not disturb it!

Color the cairn and the rules to remember.

1. Do not tamper with cairns.

If a cairn is tampered with or an unauthorized one is built, then future visitors may become disoriented or even lost.

2. Do not build unauthorized cairns.

Moving rocks disturbs the soil and makes the area more prone to erosion. Disturbing rocks can disturb fragile plants.

3. Do not add to existing cairns.

Authorized cairns are carefully designed. Adding to them can actually cause them to collapse.

Decoding Using American Sign Language

American Sign Language, also called ASL for short, is a language that many Deaf people or people who are hard of hearing use to communicate. People use ASL to communicate with their hands. Did you know people from all over the country and world travel to national parks? You may hear people speaking other languages. You might also see people using ASL. Use the American Manual Alphabet chart to decode some national parks facts.

This was the first national park to be established:

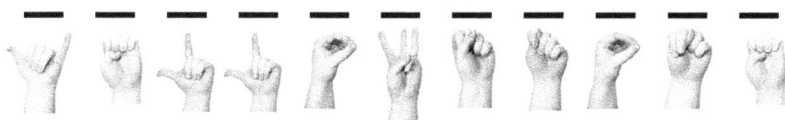

_ _ _ _ _ _ _ _ _ _

This is the biggest national park in the US:

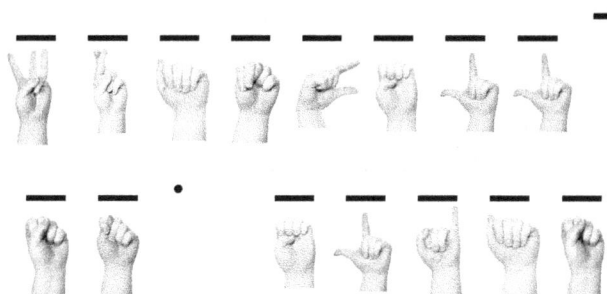

_ _ _ _ _ _ _ _ -

_ _ . _ _ _ _ _

This is the most visited national park:

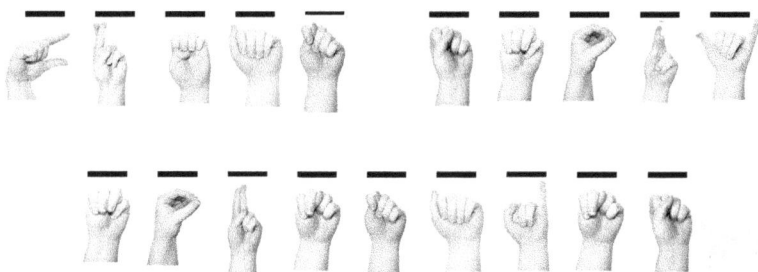

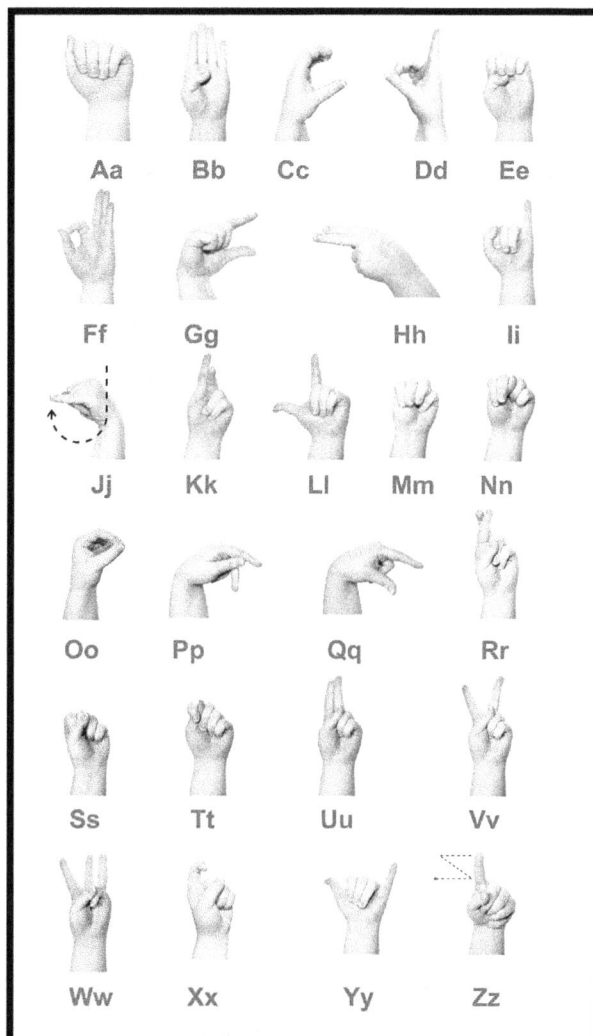

_ _ _ _   _ _ _ _ _

_ _ _ _ _ _ _ _

Aa	Bb	Cc	Dd	Ee
Ff	Gg		Hh	Ii
Jj	Kk	Ll	Mm	Nn
Oo	Pp		Qq	Rr
Ss	Tt	Uu	Vv	
Ww	Xx	Yy	Zz	

Hint: Pay close attention to the position of the thumb!

Try it! Using the chart, try to make the letters of the alphabet with your hand. What is the hardest letter to make? Can you spell out your name? Show a friend or family member and have them watch you spell out the name of the national park you are in.

Go Birdwatching at Prisoners Harbor

start here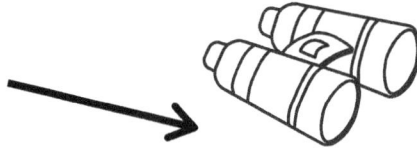

Butterflies of the Channel Isands

Species of butterflies and moths live in Channel Islands National Park. Their wingspan size varies, as do the patterns on their wings. Design your own butterfly below. Make sure the wings are symmetrical, which means both sides match.

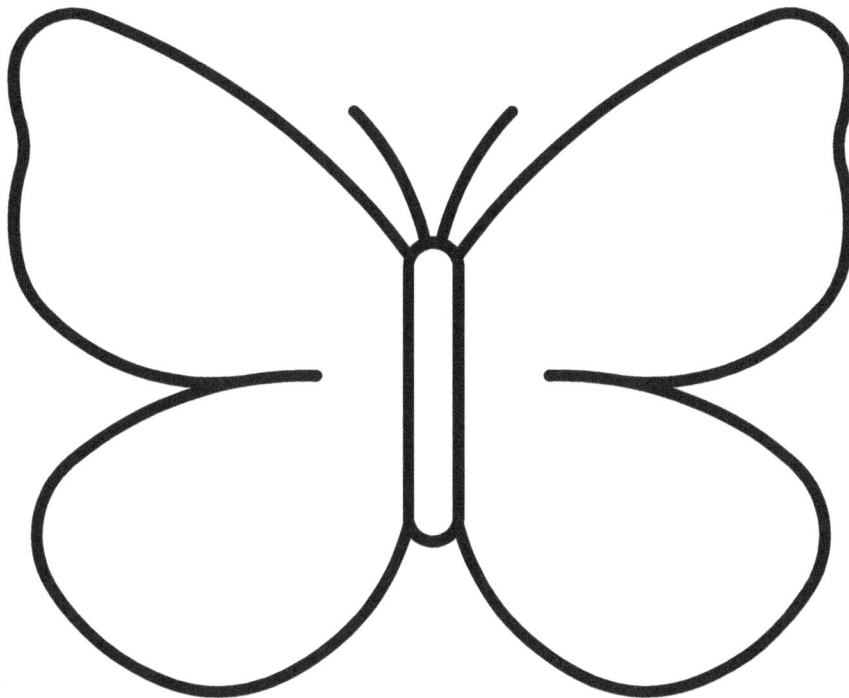

A Hike at Arch Point

Fill in the blanks on this page without looking at the full story. Once you have each line filled out, use the words you've chosen to complete the story on the next page.

ADJECTIVE _____

SOMETHING TO EAT _____

SOMETHING TO DRINK _____

NOUN _____

ARTICLE OF CLOTHING _____

BODY PART _____

VERB _____

ANIMAL _____

SAME TYPE OF FOOD _____

ADJECTIVE _____

SAME ANIMAL _____

VERB THAT ENDS IN "ED" _____

NUMBER _____

A DIFFERENT NUMBER _____

SOMETHING THAT FLIES _____

LIGHT SOURCE _____

PLURAL NOUN _____

FAMILY MEMBER _____

YOUR NICKNAME _____

A Hike at Arch Point

Use the words from the previous page to complete a silly story.

I went for a hike at Arch Point today. In my favorite _ _ _ _ _ _ _ backpack, I
ADJECTIVE

made sure to pack a map so I wouldn't get lost. I also threw in an extra

_ _ _ _ _ _ _ _ _ _ _ just in case I got hungry and a bottle of _ _ _ _ _ _ _ _ _ _ _. I put
SOMETHING TO EAT   SOMETHING TO DRINK

on my _ _ _ _ _ _ _ _ _ spray, and I tied a _ _ _ _ _ _ _ _ _ _ _ _ around my
NOUN   ARTICLE OF CLOTHING

_ _ _ _ _ _ _ _ _ _, in case it gets chilly. I started to _ _ _ _ _ _ down the path. As
BODY PART   VERB

soon as I turned the corner, I came face to face with a(n) _ _ _ _ _ _ _ _. I think
ANIMAL

it was as startled as I was! What should I do? I had to think fast! Should I

give it some of my _ _ _ _ _ _ _ _ _ _ _? No. I had to remember what the
SAME TYPE OF FOOD

_ _ _ _ _ _ _ ranger told me: "If you see one, back away slowly and try not to
ADJECTIVE

scare it." Soon enough, the _ _ _ _ _ _ _ _ _ _   _ _ _ _ _ _ _ _ _ _ away. The coast
SAME ANIMAL   VERB THAT ENDS IN ED

was clear. _ _ _ _ _ _ hours later, I finally reached the lookout. I felt like I could
NUMBER

see for a _ _ _ _ _ _ miles. I took a picture of a _ _ _ _ _ _ _ _ so I could always
A DIFFERENT NUMBER   NOUN

remember this moment. As I was putting my camera away, a _ _ _ _ _ _ _ _ _
SOMETHING THAT FLIES

flew by, reminding me that it was almost nighttime. I turned on my

_ _ _ _ _ _ _ _ _ _ and headed back. I could hear the _ _ _ _ _ _ _ _ _ _ singing their
LIGHT SOURCE   PLURAL INSECT

evening song. Just as I was getting tired, I saw my _ _ _ _ _ _ _ _ _ _ and our tent.
FAMILY MEMBER

"Welcome back _ _ _ _ _ _ _ _! How was your hike?"
NICKNAME

41

Map Symbol Sudoku

The National Park System makes park maps using symbols instead of words.
They are easily understood and take up way less space on a tiny map.

Trailhead   Waterfall   Wilderness   Campground

Complete this symbol sudoku puzzle. Fill each square with one of the symbols. Each one can appear only once in each row, column, and mini 2x2 grid. Each symbol means something, so you can write what the symbol represents instead of drawing the symbols if you prefer.

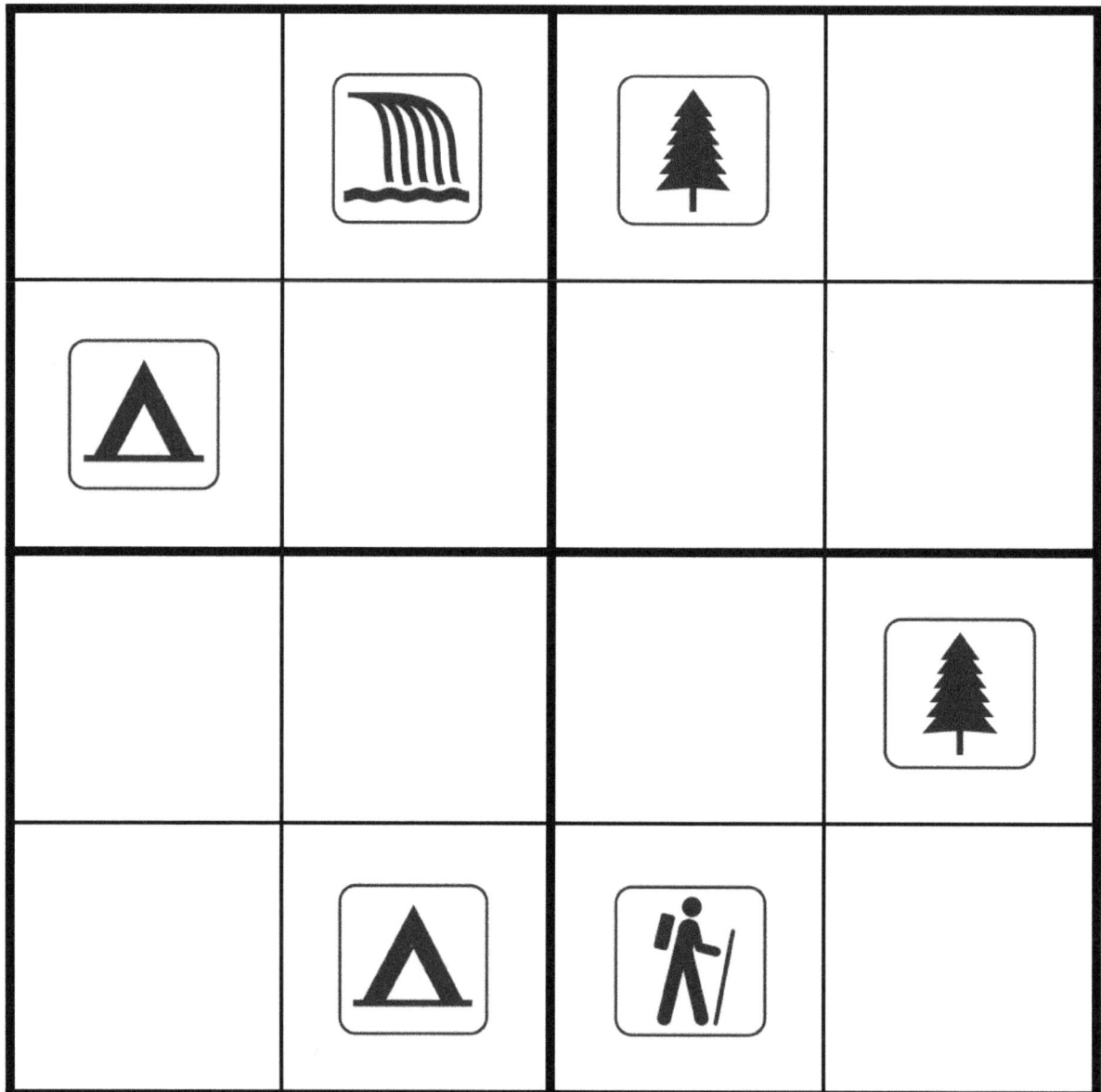

Let's Go Camping
Word Search

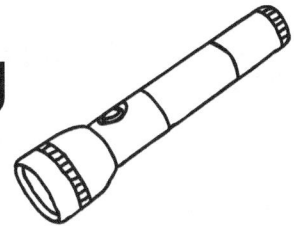

Words may be horizontal, vertical, diagonal, or they might even be backwards!

1. TENT
2. CAMP STOVE
3. SLEEPING BAG
4. BUG SPRAY
5. SUNSCREEN
6. MAP
7. FLASHLIGHT
8. PILLOW
9. LANTERN
10. ICE
11. SNACKS
12. SMORES
13. WATER
14. FIRST AID KIT
15. CHAIR
16. CARDS
17. BOOKS
18. GAMES
19. TRAIL
20. HAT

```
D P P I L L O W D B T E A C I
E O A D P R E A A M B R C A N
P W C A M P S T O V E I H X G
R A H S G E L E B E E D A P S
E L B U G S P R A Y N G I E A
S I A H G C I C N N M E R C N
C W N L A F I R S K O O B F K
M T A E M I L E L H M R W L J
T A P R E A O R E S L B A A B
S M P A S R R T E N T L U S C
C E A I I R C G P E I U J H A
S S N A C K S S I M O K I L R
I J R S F O I S N J R A Q I D
C Y E T L E V E G U O R V G S
E W T A K C A B B S S O H H M
X J N F I R S T A I D K I T T
U A A E S S E N G E T P V A B
C J L I A R T D N A M A H A S
```

All in the Day of a Park Ranger

Park Rangers are hardworking individuals dedicated to protecting our parks, monuments, museums, and more. They take care of the natural and cultural resources for future generations. Rangers also help protect the visitors of the park. Their responsibilities are broad and they work both with the public and behind the scenes.

What have you seen park rangers do? Use your knowledge of the duties of park rangers to fill out a typical daily schedule, listing one activity for each hour. Feel free to make up your own, but some examples of activities are provided on the right. Read carefully! Not all the example activities are befitting a ranger.

Time	Activity
6 am	Lead a sunrise hike
7 am	
8 am	
9 am	
10 am	
11 am	
12 pm	Enjoy a lunch break outside
1 pm	
2 pm	
3 pm	
4 pm	Teach visitors about the geology of the islands
5 pm	
6 pm	
7 pm	
8 pm	
9 pm	

- feed the migratory birds
- build trails for visitors to enjoy
- throw rocks off the side of the mountain
- rescue lost hikers
- study animal behavior
- record air quality data
- answer questions at the visitor center
- pick wildflowers
- pick up litter
- share marshmallows with the deer mice
- repair handrails
- lead a class on a field trip
- catch frogs and make them race
- lead people on educational hikes
- write articles for the park website
- protect the ocean from pollution
- remove non-native plants from the park
- study how climate change is affecting the park
- give a talk about foxes
- lead a program for campers on the California Brown Pelican

If you were a park ranger, which of the above tasks would you enjoy most?

_____

44 _____

Draw Yourself as a Park Ranger

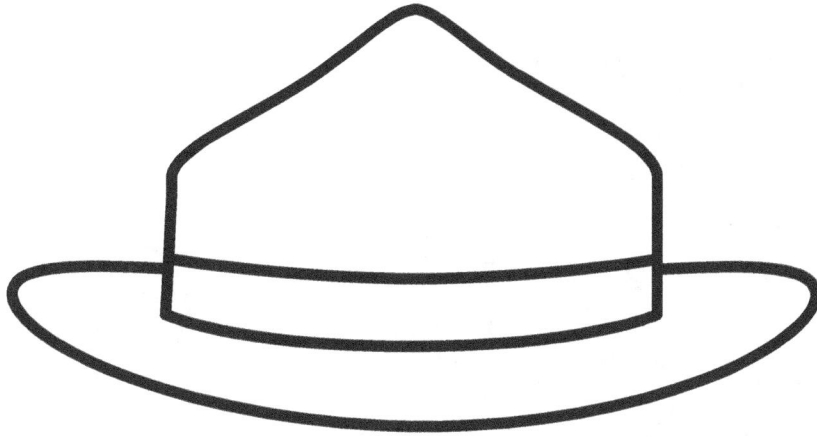

RANGER

Fish of the Channel Islands

1.

NIUGRNO

2.

HRCEP

Unscramble the common names of these fish that live in the park.

3.

OHCNAVY

4.

BGOY

5.

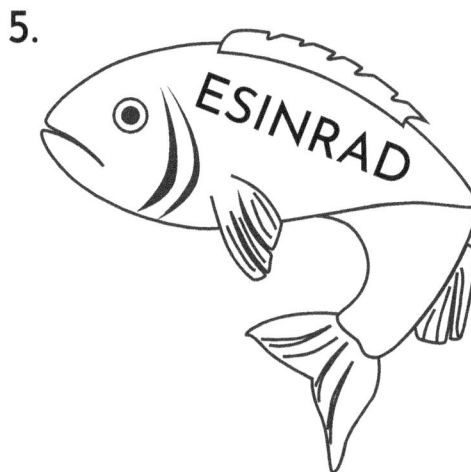

ESINRAD

1. _____
2. _____
3. _____
4. _____
5. _____

Word Bank

whitefish
sardine
anchovy
perch
goby
salmon
grunion
catfish

Amphibians

One species of frog lives in Channel Islands National Park. Even more types of salamanders live there too. In the begging of a frog's life, it starts as a tadpole. Similarly, baby salamanders are called efts. Tadpoles and efts hatch from eggs, usually in springs or pools of water.

Both frogs and salamanders are amphibians. Color the amphibians below.

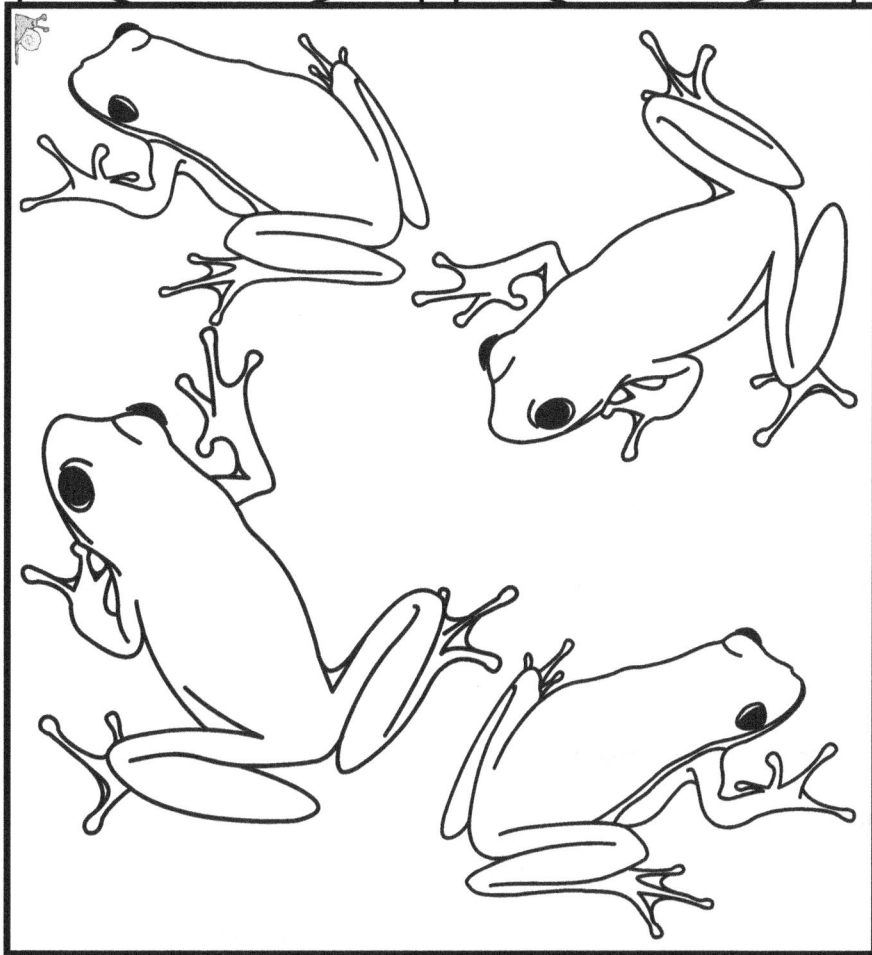

Sound Exploration

Spend a minute or two listening to all of the sounds around you.
Draw your favorite sound.

How did this sound make you feel?

_____

_____

What did you think when you heard this sound?

_____

_____

Star Messages

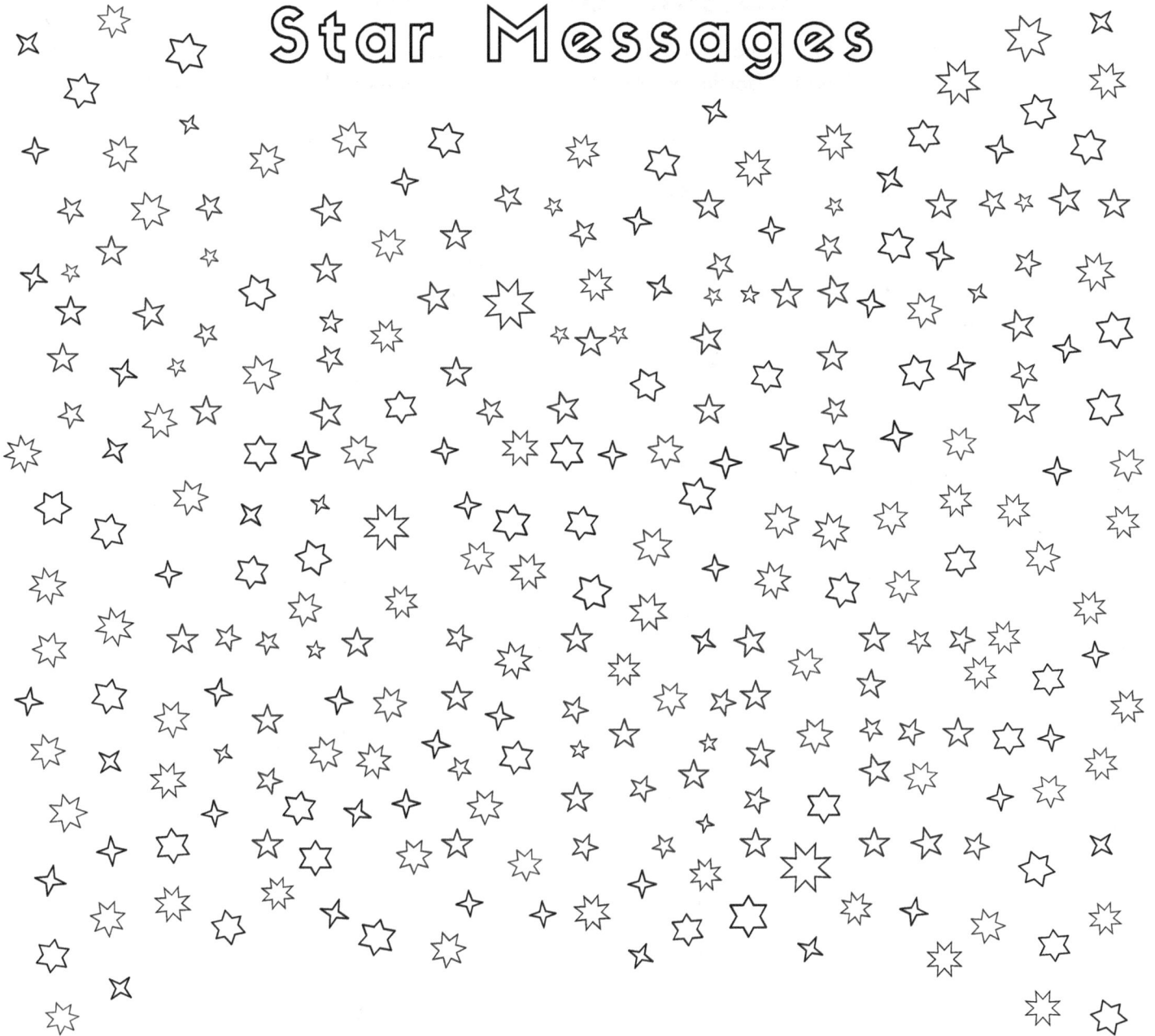

The ashy storm-petrel is an all-gray sea bird that nests in the rocky crevices along cliffs, offshore rocks, and under driftwood in sea caves.

Color in all the stars with exactly 5 points to find out when these birds hunt for squid, fish, and krill.

63 National Parks

How many other national parks have you been to? Which one do you want to visit next? Note that if some of these parks fall on the border of more than one state, you may check it off more than once!

Alaska
- ☐ Denali National Park
- ☐ Gates of the Arctic National Park
- ☐ Glacier Bay National Park
- ☐ Katmai National Park
- ☐ Kenai Fjords National Park
- ☐ Kobuk Valley National Park
- ☐ Lake Clark National Park
- ☐ Wrangell-St. Elias National Park

American Samoa
- ☐ National Park of American Samoa

Arizona
- ☐ Grand Canyon National Park
- ☐ Petrified Forest National Park
- ☐ Saguaro National Park

Arkansas
- ☐ Hot Springs National Park

California
- ☐ Channel Islands National Park
- ☐ Death Valley National Park
- ☐ Joshua Tree National Park
- ☐ Kings Canyon National Park
- ☐ Lassen Volcanic National Park
- ☐ Pinnacles National Park
- ☐ Redwood National Park
- ☐ Sequoia National Park
- ☐ Yosemite National Park

Colorado
- ☐ Black Canyon of the Gunnison National Park
- ☐ Great Sand Dunes National Park
- ☐ Mesa Verde National Park
- ☐ Rocky Mountain National Park

Florida
- ☐ Biscayne National Park
- ☐ Dry Tortugas National Park
- ☐ Everglades National Park

Hawaii
- ☐ Haleakalā National Park
- ☐ Hawai'i Volcanoes National Park

Idaho
- ☐ Yellowstone National Park

Kentucky
- ☐ Mammoth Cave National Park

Indiana
- ☐ Indiana Dunes National Park

Maine
- ☐ Acadia National Park

Michigan
- ☐ Isle Royale National Park

Minnesota
- ☐ Voyageurs National Park

Missouri
- ☐ Gateway Arch National Park

Montana
- ☐ Glacier National Park
- ☐ Yellowstone National Park

Nevada
- ☐ Death Valley National Park
- ☐ Great Basin National Park

New Mexico
- ☐ Carlsbad Caverns National Park
- ☐ White Sands National Park

North Dakota
- ☐ Theodore Roosevelt National Park

North Carolina
- ☐ Great Smoky Mountains National Park

Ohio
- ☐ Cuyahoga Valley National Park

Oregon
- ☐ Crater Lake National Park

South Carolina
- ☐ Congaree National Park

South Dakota
- ☐ Badlands National Park
- ☐ Wind Cave National Park

Tennessee
- ☐ Great Smoky Mountains National Park

Texas
- ☐ Big Bend National Park
- ☐ Guadalupe Mountains National Park

Utah
- ☐ Arches National Park
- ☐ Bryce Canyon National Park
- ☐ Canyonlands National Park
- ☐ Capitol Reef National Park
- ☐ Zion National Park

Virgin Islands
- ☐ Virgin Islands National Park

Virginia
- ☐ Shenandoah National Park

Washington
- ☐ Mount Rainier National Park
- ☐ North Cascades National Park
- ☐ Olympic National Park

West Virginia
- ☐ New River Gorge National Park

Wyoming
- ☐ Grand Teton National Park
- ☐ Yellowstone National Park

Other National Parks Crossword

Besides Channel Islands National Park, there are 62 other diverse and beautiful national parks across the United States. Try your hand at this crossword. If you need help, look at the previous page for some hints.

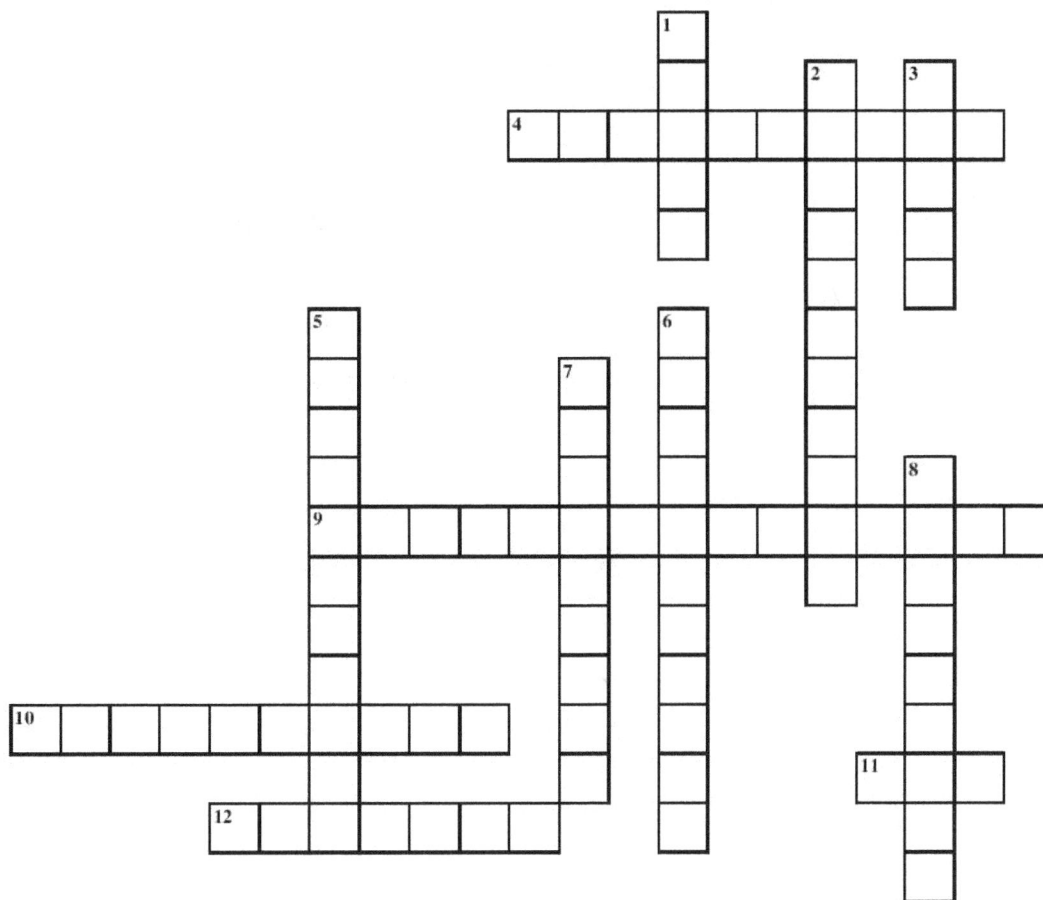

Down

1. State where Acadia National Park is located
2. This national park has the Spanish word for turtle in it
3. Number of national parks in Alaska
5. This national park has some of the hottest temperatures in the world
6. This national park is the only one in Idaho
7. This toothsome creature can famously be found in Everglades National Park
8. Only president with a national park named for them

Across

4. This state has the most national parks
9. This park has some of the newest land in the US, caused by volcanic eruptions
10. This park has the deepest lake in the United States
11. This color shows up in the name of a national park in California
12. This national park deserves a gold medal

Which National Park Will You Go To Next?
Word Search

1. ZION
2. BIG BEND
3. GLACIER
4. OLYMPIC
5. SEQUOIA
6. BRYCE
7. MESA VERDE
8. BISCAYNE
9. WIND CAVE
10. GREAT BASIN
11. KATMAI
12. YELLOWSTONE
13. VOYAGEURS
14. ARCHES
15. BADLANDS
16. DENALI
17. GLACIER BAY
18. HOT SPRINGS

```
F M M E S A V E R D E B N E Y
E A B I G B E N D E S A S E M
Y L I C A L O Y N E E D L T G
D M G A S S A U C N R L U E R
C E L I I T S C R E O A A K E
S N A W Y E E O I W T N A C A
G I C H A A Q C S E M D N S T
N O I Z P R U T I M R S N E B
I W E L M P O N B W E B K H A
R J R F D N I F L I H B U C S
P A B E E S A N E S O P W R I
S J A E N Y A C S I B A U A N
T C Y I A D O H H Y M E A L R
O T A T L M L E S E G R W R J
H S T O I K A T M A I R O P B
I C H U R C O L Y M P I C O U
O Y G T S D E O S B R Y C E T
W I N D C A V E I N R O H E M
```

Field Notes

Spend some time reflecting on your trip to Channel Islands National Park. Your field notes will help you remember the things you experienced. Use the space below to write about your day.

While I was at Channel Islands National Park...

I saw:

_____

_____

_____

_____

I heard:

_____

_____

_____

I felt:

_____

Draw a picture of your favorite thing in the park.

_____

I wondered:

_____

_____

_____

_____

_____

ANSWER KEY

Surf the Waves on Santa Rosa Island

start here →

DID YOU KNOW?

Surfing is an adventurous way to explore Channel Islands National Park. All surf spots are remote and best accessed by private boat.

Answers: Who lives here?

Below are 7 plants and animals that live in the park.
Use the word bank to fill in the clues below.

WORD BANK: GEODUCK, GRAY WHALE, OSPREY, LIMPET,
BULL KELP, VERBENA, KESTREL

L I MPET

O S PREY

BUL L ■ KELP

GR A Y ■ WHALE

VERBE N A

GEO D UCK

KE S TREL

Find the Match!
Common Names and Latin Names

Match the common name to the scientific name for each animal. The first one is done for you. Use clues on the page before and after this one to complete the matches.

Channel Island Gray Fox — Haliaeetus leucocephalus

California Sagebrush — Zalophus californianus

Island Oak — Mirounga angustirostris

California Sea Lion — Chelonia mydas

Great Horned Owl — Artemisia californica

Bald Eagle — Uta stansburiana

Northern Elephant Seal — Bubo virginianus

Green Sea Turtle — Urocyon littoralis

Side-blotched Lizard — Quercus tomentella

Bald Eagle

Haliaeetus leucocephalus

Jumbles Answers   When Nature Calls

1. BOATING

2. HIKING

3. BIRDING

4. CAMPING

5. PICNICKING

6. SIGHTSEEING

7. SNORKELING

1. recycling
2. urinate
3. ecosystem
4. flush
5. plumbing
6. pit
7. container
8. flow
9. never
10. ashes
11. hard
12. inches

National Park Emblem Answers

1. This represents all plants: **Sequoia Tree**

2. This represents all animals: **Bison**

3. This represents the landscapes: **Mountains**

4. This represents the waters protected by the park service: **Water**

5. This represents the historical and archeological values: **Arrowhead**

Answers: The Ten Essentials

Careful preparation and knowledge are key to a successful adventure to Channel Island.

The ten essentials are a list of things that are important to have when you go for longer hikes. If you go on a hike to the <u>backcountry</u>, it is especially important that you have everything you need in case of an emergency. If you get lost or something unforeseen happens, it is good to be prepared to survive until help finds you.

The ten essentials list was developed in the 1930s by an outdoors group called the Mountaineers. Over time and technological advancements, this list has evolved. Can you identify all the things on the current list? Circle each of the "essentials" and cross out everything that doesn't make the cut.

(fire: matches, lighter, tinder, and/or stove)	~~a pint of milk~~	~~extra money~~	(headlamp, plus extra batteries)	(extra clothes)
(extra water)	~~a dog~~	~~Polaroid camera~~	~~bug net~~	~~lightweight game like a deck of cards~~
(extra food)	~~a roll of duct tape~~	(shelter)	(sun protection, such as sunglasses, sun-protective clothes and sunscreen)	(knife, plus a gear repair kit)
~~a mirror~~	(navigation: map, compass, altimeter, GPS device, or satellite messenger)	(first aid kit)	~~extra flip-flops~~	~~entertainment like video games or books~~

Backcountry - a remote undeveloped rural area.

Channel Islands Word Search

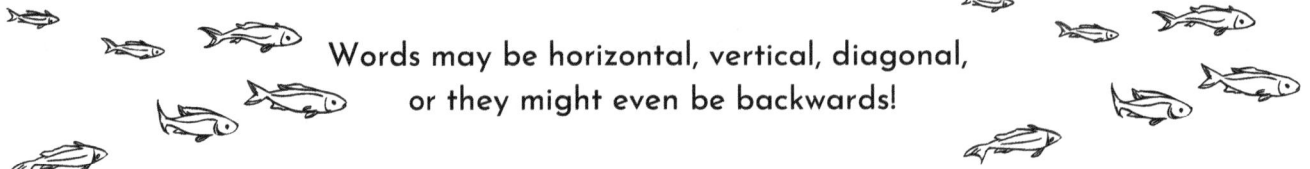

Words may be horizontal, vertical, diagonal,
or they might even be backwards!

1. MARINE
2. SEAWEED
3. SEALIONS
4. CALIFORNIA
5. FOX
6. GRASSLAND
7. CHUMASH
8. TOMOLS
9. FISHING
10. SANTA CRUZ
11. DEVILS PEAK
12. SCUBA
13. WHALE WATCH
14. STAIRCASE
15. LIZARDS
16. BOATRIDE
17. CHARTER
18. SEA
19. PACIFIC
20. CLIFFS

```
C A L I F O R N I A R E S K S
H T A T M I L E S H E R W R A
T E S E A W E E D C L B R P N
S M P A S P R U D E R L E A T
C E A I I E R N Q E I N T C A
H O L D Y W A O B I E R I O R
U O A D P L E G S R T R A F R
M W B A S E I N A W E I H I A
A A H S G E L M C E E D C C N
S L A C B O A T R I D E O T R
H R A U A C I L I Z A R D S A
G C N B K M O I A O B K G R E
I W H A L E W A T C H A N F D
J Y G T O M O L S O O R I O O
N W X A K C L I F F S O H X M
S A N T A C R U Z L Z E S Q N
U A E S E A L I O N S P I E B
D E V I L S P E A K M A F A S
```

60

Wildlife Wisdom

The national park is home to many different kinds of animals. Seeing wildlife can be an exciting part of visiting the national park but it is important to remember that these animals are wild. They need plenty of space and a healthy habitat where they can find their own food. Part of this is not allowing animals to eat any human food. This is their home and we are the visitors. We need to be respectful of the wildlife in the park.

Directions: Circle the highlighted words that best complete the following sentences.

If an animal changes its behavior because of your presence, you are:
A) too close
B) funny looking
C) dehydrated and should drink more water

The best thing we can do to help wild animals survive is:
A) make them pets
B) protect their habitat
C) knit them winter sweaters

In a national park, it is okay to share your food with wild animals:
A) never
B) always
C) sometimes

When you're hiking in an area where there are bears, you should warn bears that you are entering their space by:
A) hiking quietly
B) making noise
C) wearing bright colors

At night, park rangers care for the animals by:
A) putting them back into their cages
B) tucking them into bed
C) leaving them alone

If you see an abandoned bird's nest, it is best to:
A) pet the baby birds
B) leave it alone
C) crunch the empty eggshells

Spotted skunks forage along the ground in hopes of finding:
A) granola bars
B) Jerusalem Crickets
C) peanuts to eat

The place where an animal lives is called its:
A) condo
B) habitat
C) crib

Solution: Hike to the Beach

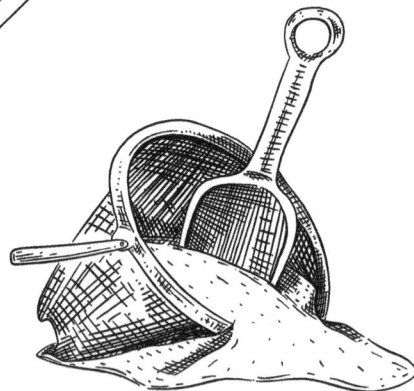

Answers: Leave No Trace Quiz

Leave No Trace is a concept that helps people make decisions during outdoor recreation that protects the environment. There are seven principles that guide us when we spend time outdoors, whether you are in a national park or not. Are you an expert in Leave No Trace? Take this quiz and find out!

1. How can you plan ahead and prepare to ensure you have the best experience you can in the National Park?

    A. Make sure you stop by the ranger station for a map and to ask about current conditions.

2. What is an example of traveling on a durable surface?

    A. Walking only on the designated path.

3. Why should you dispose of waste properly?

    C. So that other peoples' experiences of the park are not impacted by you leaving your waste behind.

4. How can you best follow the concept "leave what you find?"

    B. Take pictures but leave any physical items where they are.

5. What is not a good example of minimizing campfire impacts?

    C. Building a new campfire ring in a location that has a better view.

6. What is a poor example of respecting wildlife?

    A. Building squirrel houses out of rocks from the river so the squirrels have a place to live.

7. How can you show consideration of other visitors?

    B. Wear headphones on the trail if you choose to listen to music.

Tide Pool Word Search

A tide pool is an isolated pocket of seawater found in the intertidal's zone. They are packed with resilient sea life. Be sure to check out tide-pooling safety tips before exploring!

1. ANEMONE
2. FRENCHYS
3. TRANSITION
4. INTERTIDAL
5. URCHINS
6. SUNLIGHT
7. ALGAE
8. ROCKS
9. SMUGGLERS
10. SEA STAR
11. WAVES
12. PERIWINKLES
13. BEACH
14. BARNACLES
15. MUSSELS
16. LIMPETS
17. HIGH TIDE
18. LOW TIDE
19. BECHERS BAY

```
B E C H E R S B A Y K L U W I
H L O W T I D E R T E R R R N
T E P S E L C A N R A B C N T
S M P A S P S U C E U L H O E
C E A A L G A E S E R U I I R
B E A C H W O O V B C E N T T
R O R O C K S G A A H R S I I
P W B L M E I N G W W I K S D
P E R I W I N K L E S E S N A
E N I M A B O Y H I N G O A L
Q O A P A C I T N N S E N R N
S M N E S Y H C N E R F I T E
I E O T F G B T A H F A Q N D
J N G S I E V S S O O R V E O
N A X L K C T B S L E S S U M
X J N F A A H I G H T I D E N
U U E E R S E N N E T P V E B
S J S M U G G L E R S M A L S
```

64

Decoding Using American Sign Language

American Sign Language, also called ASL for short, is a language that many Deaf people or people who are hard of hearing use to communicate. People use ASL to communicate with their hands. Did you know people from all over the country and world travel to national parks? You may hear people speaking other languages. You might also see people using ASL. Use the American Manual Alphabet chart to decode some national parks facts.

This was the first national park to be established:

Y E L L O W S T O N E

This is the biggest national park in the US:

W R A N G E L L -

S T .   E L I A S

This is the most visited national park:

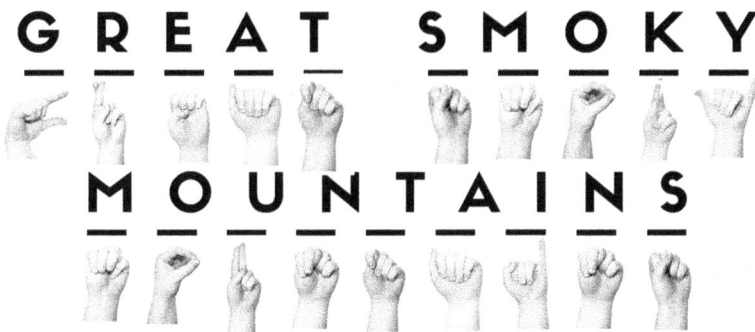

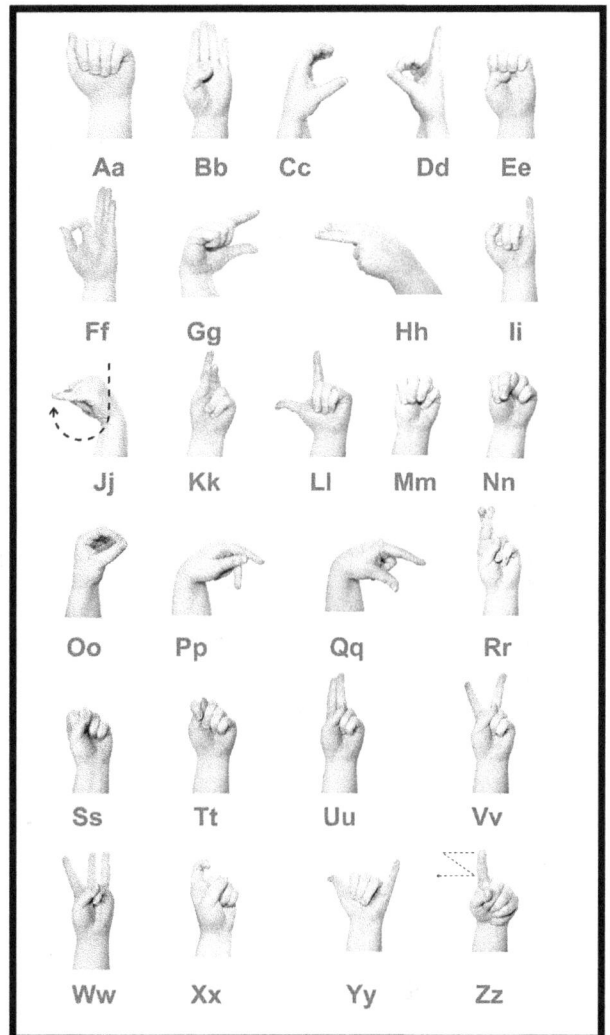

G R E A T   S M O K Y

M O U N T A I N S

Aa	Bb	Cc	Dd	Ee
Ff	Gg	Hh	Ii	
Jj	Kk	Ll	Mm	Nn
Oo	Pp	Qq	Rr	
Ss	Tt	Uu	Vv	
Ww	Xx	Yy	Zz	

Hint: Pay close attention to the position of the thumb!

Try it! Using the chart, try to make the letters of the alphabet with your hand. What is the hardest letter to make? Can you spell out your name? Show a friend or family member and have them watch you spell out the name of the national park you are in.

65

Go Birdwatching at Prisoner's Harbor

start here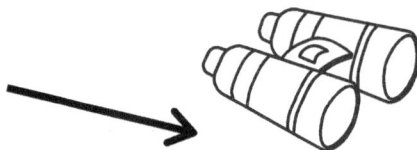

DID YOU KNOW?
Channel Islands NP is home to several birds of prey, including eagles, hawks, and owls. Birds of prey are birds that hunt other animals for food.

Map Symbol Sudoku Anwers

hiker	waterfall	tree	tent
tent	tree	waterfall	hiker
waterfall	hiker	tent	tree
tree	tent	hiker	waterfall

Let's Go Camping
Word Search

1. tent
2. camp stove
3. sleeping bag
4. bug spray
5. sunscreen
6. map
7. flashlight
8. pillow
9. lantern
10. ice
11. snacks
12. smores
13. water
14. first aid kit
15. chair
16. cards
17. books
18. games
19. trail
20. hat

```
D P P I L L O W D B T E A C I
E O A D P R E A A M B R C A N
P W C A M P S T O V E I H X G
R A H S G E L E B E E D A P S
E L B U G S P R A Y N G I E A
S I A H G C I C N N M E R C N
C W N L A F I R S K O O B F K
M T A E M I L E L H M R W L J
T A P R E A O R E S L B A A B
S M P A S R R T E N T L U S C
C E A I I R C G P E I U J H A
S S N A C K S S I M O K I L R
I J R S F O I S N J R A Q I D
C Y E T L E V E G U O R V G S
E W T A K C A B B S S O H H M
X J N F I R S T A I D K I T T
U A A E S S E N G E T P V A B
C J L I A R T D N A M A H A S
```

68

All in the Day of a Park Ranger

There are many right answers for this activity, but not all of the provided examples are good activities for a park ranger. In fact, a park ranger's job may include stopping visitors from doing some of these things.

The list below are activities that rangers do not do:

feed the migratory birds

throw rocks off the side of the mountain

pick wildflowers

share marshmallows with the deer mice

catch frogs and make them race

Fish of Channel Islands

1. GRUNION
2. PERCH
3. ANCHOVY
4. GOBY
5. SARDINE

Answers: Other National Parks Crossword

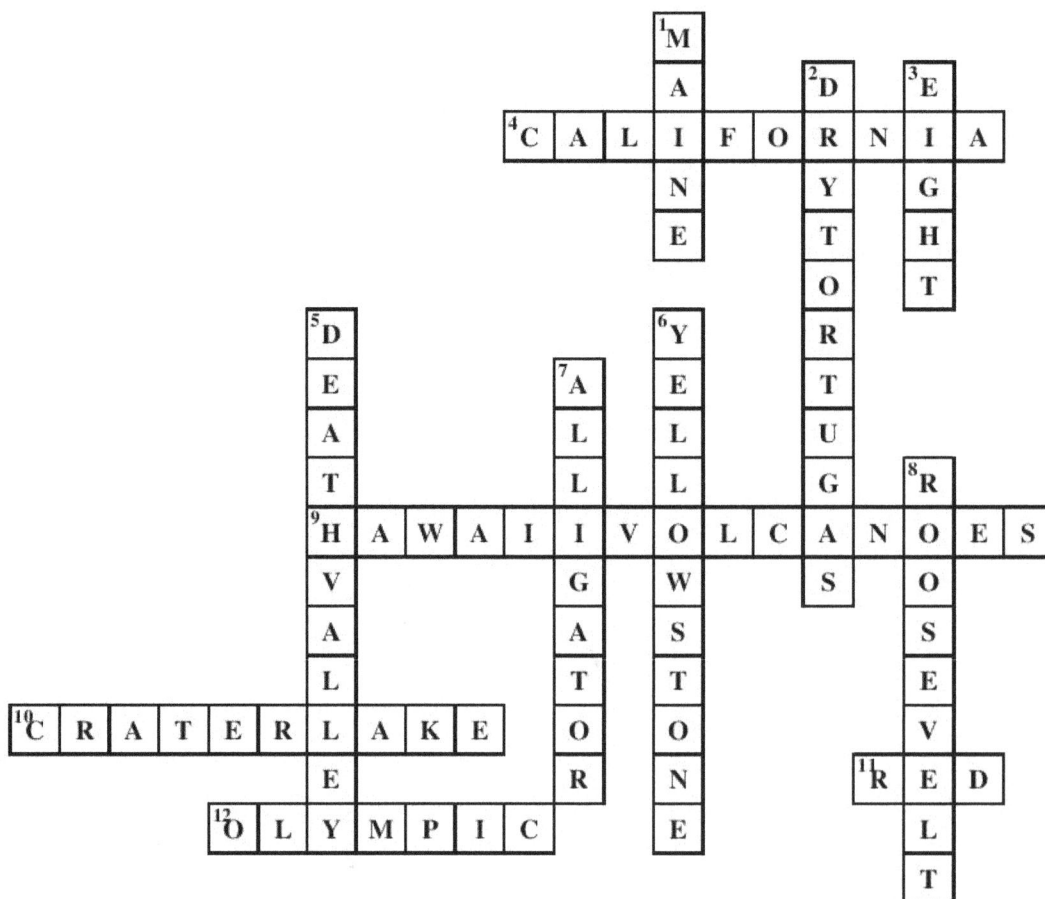

```
              ¹M
               A            ²D        ³E
      ⁴C  A  L  I  F  O  R  N  I  A
               N            Y         G
               E            T         H
                            O         T
      ⁵D                    R    ⁶Y
       E            ⁷A       T     E
       A             L             L  L
       T             L             L  L        ⁸R
      ⁹H  A  W  A  I  I  V  O  L  C  A  N  O  E  S
       V             G             W     S     O
       A             A             S           S
       L             T             T           E
     ¹⁰C  R  A  T  E  R  L  A  K  E          V
       E             O             O     ¹¹R  E  D
      ¹²O  L  Y  M  P  I  C        N           L
                                   E           T
```

Down

1. State where Acadia National Park is located
2. This National Park has the Spanish word for turtle in it
3. Number of National Parks in Alaska
5. This National Park has some of the hottest temperatures in the world
6. This National Park is the only one in Idaho
7. This toothsome creature can famously be found in Everglades National Park
8. Only president with a national park named for them

Across

4. This state has the most National Parks
9. This park has some of the newest land in the US, caused by a volcanic eruption
10. This park has the deepest lake in the United States
11. This color shows up in the name of a National Park in California
12. This National Park deserves a gold medal

Answers: Which National Park Will You Go To Next?

1. Zion
2. Big Bend
3. Glacier
4. Olympic
5. Sequoia
6. Bryce
7. Mesa Verde
8. Biscayne
9. Wind Cave
10. Great Basin
11. Katmai
12. Yellowstone
13. Voyageurs
14. Arches
15. Badlands
16. Denali
17. Glacier Bay
18. Hot Springs

```
F M M E S A V E R D E B N E Y
E A B I G B E N D E S A S E M
Y L I C A L O Y N E E D L T G
D M G A S S A U C N R L U E R
C E L I I T S C R E O A A K E
S N A W Y E E O I W T N A C A
G I C H A A Q C S E M D N S T
N O I Z P R U T I M R S N E B
I W E L M P O N B W E B K H A
R J R F D N I F L I H B U C S
P A B E E S A N E S O P W R I
S J A E N Y A C S I B A U A N
T C Y I A D O H H Y M E A L R
O T A T L M L E S E G R W R J
H S T O I K A T M A I R O P B
I C H U R C O L Y M P I C O U
O Y G T S D E O S B R Y C E T
W I N D C A V E I N R O H E M
```

LITTLE BISON

Press

Little Bison Press is an independent children's book publisher based in the Pacific Northwest. We promote exploration, conservation, and adventure through our books. Established in 2021, our passion for outside spaces and travel inspired the creation of Little Bison Press.

We seek to publish books that support children in learning about and caring for the natural places in our world.

To learn more, visit:
www.littlebisonpress.com

Want more free games and activities? Visit our website!